David O'Malley

TRUST THE ROAD

D0766488

Don Bosco Publications

ISBN 0-9544539-4-8
© Don Bosco Publications
Thornleigh House
Bolton BL1 6PQ
Tel. 01204 308 811
Fax 01204 306 868

Printed in Germany

Contents

Prayers for the Road 79

Introduction

The road of life unfolds each day in familiar patterns, new challenges and opportunities. Sometimes the pattern works out beautifully, at other times it makes as much sense as a game of snakes and ladders. Plans, relationships, work and choices all combine to make each life a unique journey. For Christians the challenge is to trust the road however it twists and turns.

Christians believe that, in the ordinary moments of each life, God is walking alongside each person. The goodness of God is locked into every life, and the gifts each person needs for their journey are already within them or available along the road ahead. The road takes each of us through time, but it is also eternal. The road takes us outwards, into a challenging world, but also leads us inwards, into who we really are. The road will take us out of ourselves, but deeper into relationship with others and the whole of creation.

This book is an encouragement to trust your road. It comes from a Salesian tradition, inspired by the gentle humanism of St Francis de Sales. He would encourage you to trust the goodness within you and in those around you. Trust the tug of that mysterious presence within. Walk hand in hand with that hidden

God who knows the road even when it goes towards the cross and through to new life.

Each of the experiences described in this book are moments on the road. Like the disciples who met Jesus walking with them after his resurrection, may your heart recognise God walking alongside you as you trust the road that lies ahead.

The Problem with Work

It was only a summer job in an electrical warehouse, but they shouldn't have treated me like that. The hourly rate was poor and the verbal abuse I got from the permanent staff made me feel like dirt under their feet. It was like being bullied at school all over again, but this time there were no school staff to sort it out. "Put up and shut up or get out," said the boss, so I did. But each day what confidence I had grew weaker, I was less certain about conversations and more isolated. Each day I became more angry about the situation and yet I felt like crying at the same time. The other permanent staff just sat and laughed as I worked through the coffee breaks and became a virtual slave. In the end I gave the job up, but not without making my mark on that firm. Just after I picked up my wages I got back on the forklift and moved one last stack of videos, only I didn't get the pallet quite right and let the whole lot crash to the floor. In the uproar and cursing that followed I disappeared never to return.

Looking back I realised I was just being childish and going down to their level and I wished I hadn't done it. But injustice breeds injustice and today, working in my own business, I make sure that people are treated with justice and dignity. I make sure I am around to see what is going on and I try to create a friendly spirit in the workplace. I feel I am building a better, safer and more just society. My gospel belief helps me support each person's dignity.

LORD,
you recognise the dignity of each person,
you even spent time with very small children,
everyone mattered to you.
In the world of work
it often seems that I am a cog in a machine;
something that can be thrown away when worn out.
Help me Lord to resist the supremacy of economics
which tries to measure everything by profit and loss.
Help me to value every individual
not only by the work they do
but also by the relationships and community they build,
for, in working well, I am helping to create a better world.
Help me to recognise your presence in the things I do
and the people I work with.
Then I can work with dignity, and equality
with my brothers and sisters in the workplace.

Who are my Real Friends?

I sat slumped in my bedroom smouldering with anger. What are friends for I thought, to use you or dominate you? This wasn't the first time my so-called friends had stood me up, cut me out and didn't have time to listen. Almost automatically I reached for my dictionary, a present from dad for passing my end of year exams. I thumbed through to friendship and looked for the origin of the word. There it was, as clear as day, it said that friend was an old word in some languages, describing someone who sets you free. That's why I felt so upset now; my friends, rather than setting me free, were trapping me in their plans, dumping me when they felt like it and were not at all interested in the real me.

Of course I wasn't stupid enough to think I was a perfect friend either. I had dropped people and pressurised them into doing what I wanted. But here today in my anger I realised how damaging that could be. Looking at friendship as setting someone free set me looking at my other relationships again. John for example always remembered to ask how I was feeling – but never made fun of me. Sue always praised my successes and she was the one who would be deadly honest about how I looked. Yet until now I had not thought of Sue or John as friends. Come to think of it, when they were around I did feel more relaxed, more myself and somehow safe. I realised that somehow people like Sue and John set the goodness of people free. Their respect and listening and honesty made it easier to see God in ordinary people. I never saw Sue or John in the same way again.

LORD,
I want to be a good friend, honest, caring, fun to be with.
I want to be listened to and respected as well.
I need to know myself better and trust people.
Lord, how do I make and keep good friends?
People move in and out of my life
like shoppers in a supermarket.
How do I know who I can trust?
I get so enthusiastic about something
and when someone laughs I feel like a fool.
Where do I get the courage to be myself?
Where do I find friends who will accept me just as I am?

I know that the Christian story tells us
to make the first move.
I need to keep trusting, reaching out in friendship.
Faith for me right now is believing in me,
my goodness, my own mystery.
Stay with me Lord as I look into the eyes of others,
and help me to recognise your face in them.

In that way all my friendships will be based
on your presence,
discovering your mystery, living in other people.

TRY NOT TO COMPLAIN ABOUT THE SMALL INSULTS
YOU RECEIVE. BECAUSE THE ONE WHO COMPLAINS
OFTEN FEELS THE INSULT TO BE GREATER THAN IT
ACTUALLY IS.

St Francis de Sales

Making Decisions

I didn't mean to shout at my well-meaning friend – she didn't deserve it. Anyway, how could I expect her to know the answers when I didn't. The question of what I wanted to do in life was one that only I could answer and the loneliness of that choice was the cause of my frustration.

How am I supposed to decide such huge things? I was often told that I had a gift with people, a really warm and friendly approach. I glowed inside when I heard people say that. Going into education, and maybe even overseas volunteering, therefore seemed the natural step. But I also had a physics teacher who kept on telling me I had what it takes to do pure science and was potentially the brightest scientific mind he'd ever taught, and he was near retirement! I enjoyed science, but I found it hard to believe what Mr James, my physics teacher, said. "Don't waste what you've got. If you want to help people do it through science – it's your best gift."

I knew people were called through their gifts and he knew I was being called by two different gifts in two different directions and the choice had to be made in the next two weeks! I sat in my room, thinking it through, agonising, praying and not getting any answers. The only advice that meant anything to me was my Grandmother's: "Follow your bliss," she said mysteriously and just smiled. I sat and talked to God, searched for my bliss, and in those uncertain choices I began to claim responsibility for my own life journey. I took the first faltering adult steps into a shared pilgrimage with the spirit of God within me.

LORD,
you don't make it easy!
There's too many ways to go
and a dozen reasons for each way.
Life seems like a game of snakes and ladders,
because if I make the wrong choice
I'm back where I started.
Then again if I climb the ladders,
am I just showing off, or joining the rat race?
Some of my friends seem so sure where they're going,
their confidence scares me.
They climb the nearest ladder
and don't seem to see the snakes.
But life isn't a game Lord, this is my life, my choice.
I have to make the choices
and live with the consequences.
I know that Lord.
Just stay with me whatever happens.
Make sense of what doesn't work out.

Help me to touch some of that wisdom,
that you have buried deep in my heart.
Help me to follow my bliss,
and pay the price as you did.
That was your cross to your resurrection miracle.

WHEN WE REALLY DON'T KNOW WHAT TO DO,
WHEN NO ANSWERS COME FROM ANY DIRECTION,
THEN IT IS THEN THAT GOD INSPIRES US.

St Francis de Sales

Tonight he said he loved me

He said it tonight but I had seen it in his face for weeks. He loves me. It was such a relief to finally name something that had happened to us weeks and weeks ago. I remember a teacher, the year I left school, telling me that falling in love was like walking on air for days and days. I called him an old romantic and privately thought he was wired up to the moon! Tonight I changed my mind. He said tonight that he loves me and I know it's true because I'm walking on air!

Its not that he's good looking or seen as a bit of a catch by others. He's just himself, and when he's with me I feel more myself than ever before. It's not even that we've gone the distance with touch, but somehow it feels deeper than touching. Not that touch hasn't been a big part of our relationship. It's more that I feel absolutely safe with him and yet totally vulnerable too. He said he loved me and it was as if we had come home to each other. We belong together.

I looked right into his eyes as he said the words. The courage to find the best way to say it, the desperation to know how I would react were both written in neon lights across his face. I waited for that word love to be said into the space between us. There it was hanging in the air between our faces and I sighed a smile at him, relaxed into his arms, and said, "Yes, me too." It was a relief to get to this point and celebrate together because both of us had heard that word love before in relationships without the meaning and commitment it carries. I think both of us had been hanging back from using it because we knew what it might mean. Tonight we both recognised the sacredness of that moment when we admitted that we had found a home in each others lives.

TONIGHT

he said he loved me.
Lord, your love is powerful stuff!
I can see why the scriptures tell us that God is Love.
Thank you for this energy
and sense of connection to all of life.

Tonight he said he loved me.
Knowing that I'm loved has changed my life
and turned me upside down.
Yet I know friends and family have loved me for years.
Why is this so different Lord?
Maybe it's because it didn't have to be said out of duty.
Maybe it's because he needs me as much as I need him.
Maybe too it's because in seeing each other

we have caught a glimpse of your love
living in each other.
Right now I don't even want to think about it too much.
I just want to enjoy and explore its mystery.

Tonight he said he loved me.
I want to walk on air a little longer!
But stay with us both Lord.
Be the God of love at the heart of our relationship.
Keep us safe
and help us make our home in each other's lives
as you have made your home in ours.

EYES SPEAK TO EYES AND HEART TO HEART
AND ONLY THOSE WHO LOVE
CAN UNDERSTAND WHAT IS SAID.

St Francis de Sales

My best friend became a Dad today

He's totally confused. He's a Dad and he's proud of it from his macho haircut down to his size ten feet. There are tears in his eyes and he's buying drinks for everyone. I hope he has a lot more children! I can see him trying to be tough and literally shrug it off as he talks to the barman. But as he turns around I can see the pride glowing like a nuclear reactor inside him. He keeps talking about it, describing his new tiny daughter to anyone who will listen. My best friend has changed a lot.

Later on that night I drove him back to his place for a coffee and he showed me the cot and the clothes waiting for the return of mother and daughter from hospital. We sat and talked about the wonder of it all. What would this baby turn out to be? What kind of dad would he want to be in the years ahead? For a few minutes we sat in silence, soaking up this new sense of responsibility that was seeping into his life. Adjusting to a new focus that was already more important than anything else that had happened.

I sat thinking about how he had changed over the last few weeks. The worry, the false alarms and the increasing need to be at home, all marked the beginning of a new adventure in his life. The sports club tough man had been tamed by a little baby. It was his own Christmas story, a difficult birth at a tough time with all the uncertainty of what it might mean. But it was a new birth for him too. Something new was born in him that night, a new pride, a new gentleness and determination to live out his responsibilities. I was immensely proud of him and equally envious of the joy and peace he radiated that night when he became a Dad.

LORD,
I spent half my adolescence criticising my parents,
and soon I'll be one myself.
It's a confusing life Lord.
In some ways I can't wait to hold a child of my own,
and yet it scares me too.
This world seems full of dangers and dodgy characters.
Disease violence and pollution are everywhere.
I will be responsible for my child's safety.
I know that being a mum or dad isn't just a job.
It's a relationship to be lived,
as the baby grows into the adult.
As a parent I will need to support new life
without crushing it.
I will need to encourage without railroading,
and I will make mistakes.
Just as my parents made mistakes,

and we learnt together.
Lord, you encouraged us to call God our Father,
help me to be a good parent to my children.
Maybe in doing that I will get to know you better.
Maybe I will feel even closer to you, the God of life,
the mystery at the heart of every new life and mine.

TRY TO WALK IN THE COMPANIONSHIP OF FAMILY
AND FRIENDS, GENTLY, PEACEFULLY AND WITH
LOVING KINDNESS.

St Francis de Sales

Where has he gone?

The coffin was just a box now, perched on two trestles in the middle of the church aisle. I kept telling myself that I would see him again and pick up where we had left off. But he was gone, for me he was not in that coffin at all.

He was my first boyfriend and I had loved him with all the joy and passion I had. Yet now I felt frozen and ashamed that hardly a tear had fallen from my eyes. Concerned and knowing faces surrounded me, but it seemed as if they were on a distant cinema screen with the sound turned off.

I tried to pray. "Where is he Lord? What have you done with him?" He was so good, he was a great laugh and his life didn't deserve an ending like this. I know that he showed off with his new motorbike and got a real buzz from its speed. But he didn't deserve the accident. "Where is he Lord? What have you done with him?" Will our lives ever touch again. I need someone, I need some time to make sense of this.

I felt the arm first as she slipped into the bench beside me. Claire just looked at me for a moment and knew everything. Friends like that are rare. She never said a word, but she cried for me during the service. All through the service I felt her arm around me and I clung to it for my very life. As the priest gently reassured us with words of hope and resurrection, I saw John again in my mind. He was sitting on his bike, his mop of hair blowing in the breeze over his quiet smile. In that moment I knew with certainty that love was stronger than death. I knew I would see him again. Then I cried myself, the first of many healing tears.

LORD,
I heard at school
that St Francis described death as his sister.
As if death were some sort of friend!
I don't understand that at all.
The worst thing about a death
is the hole it leaves in your life.
For a start you hardly realise how much you care
until it's too late.
All those links gone, of love and laughter,
of life and friends.
Where are they now?
I feel like Mary Magdalene
who went looking for her friend Jesus.
She was so blinded with grief,
that when she bumped into Jesus,
she didn't even recognise him.
"They have taken him away." She kept saying,

Now I know how she felt.
Jesus just had to say her name: "Mary."
Then she knew him and everything changed for her.
So speak my name Lord and let me know
that love is stronger than death.
Help me to hang on to you, the one who beat death
and brought new life that lasts forever.

NOTHING CAN EVER REALLY SEPARATE THOSE
WHOM GOD HAS JOINED IN LOVE

St Francis de Sales

Aliens!

It was the cheapest holiday I had ever had and it was guaranteed to offer ten days of sunshine. Getting on the plane for the four hours flight was really exciting. I'd never been out of Western Europe and it seemed to me the adventure of a lifetime. Leaving the ground on the last flight of the day I felt like a real world citizen. I was going to another continent for a few days relaxation and I was doing it all alone!

On arrival the blast of heat hit me through the aeroplane door. I headed down the steps through the crowd to the terminal. Inside a man whom I assumed was a policeman pushed me to the left. He jabbed his finger at a multilingual sign that indicated that I was an alien and had to go into a separate line.

How did he know I was an alien? I thought to myself as I stood in the queue. Then, looking around I began to see why: I was the only light skinned person in the terminal. I noticed people glancing at me with undisguised curiosity, some with expressions that didn't look too friendly. Suddenly my adventure looked a bit thin and the idea of relaxation went out of the terminal window. I instinctively reached for my wallet and checked the zip on my hand luggage. Then I felt ashamed for doing it. Here I was, an alien in another country, surrounded by people I expected to speak my language and yet, without reason, I mistrusted them.

I began to realise how the immigrant communities must feel in my own country. I began to understand why they have to stick together. I saw too, in a new way, how much they have achieved in travelling to a new country, learning a new language, and surviving in an alien culture. Stood in the terminal that warm humid night I realised that I was prejudiced and the real adventure into another culture might only begin when I return home to my own multi-cultural town.

LORD,
I try to be an optimist and I try to be fair,
but sometimes I am caught out in prejudice
against people who are different from me.
I notice the way I speak more now:
"He's from the Harvest estate, but he's OK!"
In saying that I condemn most people on the estate.
"She must be fifty now, but she's still a laugh!"
As if all older people are boring and miserable.
Lord, you made us different, men and women,
young and old.
Different cultures different traditions.
The variety is supposed to enrich us,
and yet it scares us.

*We look at the externals, the clothes, the food, the
gestures.
But you ask us to look deeper:
to see the potential friend,
the person in need
the one who can help our culture develop more wisely.
Lord, keep reminding me that there is no one,
who does not carry the common mark of your life living
in them.
Help me connect with you living in them.
Maybe then I will really become a world citizen.*

IN THE BUSYNESS OF YOUR DAY
KEEP AN EYE ON GOD.
BE LIKE SAILORS, WHO, GET TO THE HARBOUR
BY LOOKING TO THE STARS AS WELL AS
LOOKING AT WHERE THEY ARE ON THEIR JOURNEY.

St Francis de Sales

Hard Times

We watched as our son slipped away from us.
His bedroom became a no-go area.
His TV and music masked a deeper silence in his
soul.
He seemed like a gold fish in a bowl of darkness,
going round in circles in his mind and always deeper.
Our words were charged with love and support,
our eyes and arms longed to connect and support.
But no emotions seemed to penetrate
his Teflon defences.
Our love and concern slid off him,
to be trodden into the carpet,
as he walked back to his room.
Then it happened,
the thing we were powerless to stop:
the self-destructing overdose,
the medics the trauma.
We were scared to death.
Then, back at home it suddenly happened,
like switching on a light.
He was back with us!
No really there! To be talked with and touched.
I could feel his heart and he could feel mine!
That means a hell of a lot to a Dad.

LORD,
It's the anniversary today,
and I still don't know why I did it.
But now I'm glad my attempt at suicide failed.
It had been a tough year,
but taking those tablets! What was I thinking of?
I don't know how I got to that point.
My parents knew I was struggling,
but their concern never seemed to touch me.
My friends were cheerful and positive,
I knew they were there, but I never felt their presence.

The bedroom became my prison.
I pretended I was reading, or watching TV,
as my mind was lost in dark twists.
I believed that if I could just sort things out in my mind,
then I could also sort things out in my life outside.
In fact it's the other way around,
by starting to fix a few of those outside things,
I began to cope better with what was going on inside me.
I remember an old priest telling me: The problem before
you is never as great as the wisdom within you.
I think about that a lot now.
It gives me a bit more confidence.
After recovering I found that the disaster in my work did
happen, but I coped.
In fact I was relieved when I got the sack.

I've also met someone special,
and I think it could be the one to last a lifetime.
Thanks Lord for my parents.
Help me to love life and live it as a gift for another year.

WHATEVER WE ARE DOING,
EVEN IF WE ARE FAST ASLEEP,
WE ARE JOINED TO
THE HOLINESS OF GOD'S PRESENCE.

St Francis de Sales

The Voting card

They're all a bunch of crooks. My Dad's been saying it for years. Besides, we've always voted the same way in our family. It doesn't make any difference who's in power. So why do I find myself hoping again that things might be different this time?

It's easy to give in to pessimism I suppose, and those who are most cynical are often the ones with the most disappointed hopes. When I look back on health and safety laws, votes for all, appropriate support for the disabled, I realise things do change for the better.

Those changes happened because a lot of good people began to work together, in pressure groups and political parties. Those Justice and Peace issues are what Jesus meant by his Kingdom, a place where people's dignity would be respected and where the mystery of God living in people would be recognised.

My vote might help to build that Kingdom and it's worth hoping it just might make a difference.

LORD,
who are these people who risk their ideals
trying to change the world for the better?
If I believe the local talk in the pub I would say

they are self-serving hypocrites
who like the sound of their own voices.
But if I take a moment,
I realise many of them are the idealists
who want to make a difference,
and help build a better world.
Some lose their way and start feathering their own nest,
but most don't, they dedicate themselves to serving their
people with hardworking honest integrity.
Those who exercise authority on our behalf
deserve to be challenged, checked and scrutinised,
but they also deserve our respect, hope and confidence,
if they are to find the energy to continue to build God's
Kingdom.
The way I use my vote might help that happen.

BEING HUMAN MEANS BEING REASONABLE.
BUT BECAUSE WE ARE ALL IMPERFECT
IT IS A RARE TREASURE TO FIND
A TRULY REASONABLE PERSON.

St Francis de Sales

Speeding Ticket

I was pulled over by a police motorcyclist. It had to happen when my friends were in the car. The window was wound down, a neutral voice said, "Could I ask you to step out of the car sir?"

All my friends pushed their grinning faces against the car window, as I fumbled for my license and then, worst of all, blew into the breathalyser. I got back into the car in confusion amidst backslapping and comments, clutching a police note that could make me a criminal. But I was glad, deep down, glad that there were limits to speed and to drinking. My best friend had been run over by a drunk when he was only twelve and he is still in pain ten years later. That can't be right can it? So while I accepted the comments of Bad Luck and The police are picking on us. I was quietly grateful and mumbled, "They're just doing their job."

LORD
it's hard to learn that we have to live within limits.
There's no freedom without limits,
my old teacher used to say.
He said there was a difference between freedom from something
and freedom for something.

Left to ourselves, in our own little world,
limits wouldn't seem so important
but to live, love and work with others,
 there need to be rules.
The way I drive a car might ruin someone else's life.
The way I drink or smoke might ruin my family or job.
I need others to respect the rules too.
I have to trust that the bus-driver
or airline pilot has not been drinking.
I have to trust that my bank is honest,
in looking after my money.
That's why we need these rules to keep us all in line.
Jesus had one golden rule,
treat others as you would wish to be treated yourself.
I was speeding, I was caught and treated fairly.

WHEN A MISTAKE HAPPENS WE SHOULD CORRECT IT
WITH GENTLE CALMNESS, WITH MORE COMPASSION
THAN WITH ANGER AND THEN ENCOURAGE CHANGE
FOR THE BETTER.

St Francis de Sales

Buying Our First Home

We sat in the building society office feeling confused
at the questions we were being asked.
Have we got our payslips for the last six months?
What sort of job contracts do we have?
Can they see our bank statements?
   That was bad enough but it got worse.
Would we like to have a ten year mortgage or a
twenty five year mortgage?
What would happen if we died, would we want
insurance?
   We felt as if our whole lives were being unrolled
and analysed by a cold-hearted monster, just because
we wanted to buy our first house. I began to feel
uncomfortable.
   My partner and I had decided it was time to put
our salaries into something more than rent and admit
that our days of being flexible and drifting were
coming to an end. Sometimes that feels good and
moments later it seems like the end of life. In our
worst moments this mortgage feels like a millstone.
In our best moments it feels like a foundation stone
where we can deal with life and love and build a
home. We smiled at each other anxiously before we
signed and then went out for a drink.

LORD,
why do foundation stones so often feel like millstones?
Why does security always carry responsibility?
I suppose buying a house marks the end of a stage of life,
just as it marks the beginning of a new direction.
So, what do I want this home to be?
I want it to be our home and express who we are.
I want it to be solid and unchanging, reliable and safe.
I would like it to record the memories of our journey
and be a place with a warm atmosphere.
I'd like it to have a kind of presence around it; a place of
peace, a place of welcome and even a bit of mystery.
Most of all I want you, Lord, to bless it and fill it with
your presence.
Greet everyone who comes through the door and let them
see your presence.
Scripture calls you the keystone of the building. Be the
keystone of our new home and help us deal with the
millstone this mortgage feels like just now.

REMEMBER GOD'S PRESENCE AS OFTEN AS YOU CAN
AND NOTICE WHAT GOD IS DOING AND WHAT YOU
ARE DOING.

St Francis de Sales

Marriage!

I've watched weddings on the television soaps. They have a great tension-filled build up, a wild party and you know that they will probably split up within two years. Does that mean marriage is a waste of time or just boring? I don't think it is, because I've watched some of my friends fall in love and when they marry they just get interested in different things, babies home building and especially each other. They develop a different focus, they become more generous and less self-centred. At least that's what I've seen. I envy that shared living and responsibility. All I have to live for is me, and I feel somehow incomplete. Yet I don't know if I want to give up the independence I have. Marriage means growing into a deeper freedom, in order to be close to one other person forever. I know I am not ready to take that step right now, but I want to make it one day. I want to get out of this solo world and belong first and forever to someone else. I want to risk giving myself and living for somebody else.

LORD,
I know it's different this time,
there's a sureness about us.
I have never felt like this before.

I feel safe, feel I can be myself.
I'm not walking on air, and I have no illusions.
Yet there is a hugely romantic feel to our relationship too.
Already I find myself thinking for two,
thinking us not me.
Sometimes I get frightened
at just how close and interdependent we are.
I feel that maybe I am losing myself in this relationship,
as well as finding myself at the same time.
I am confused.
But I know that new life and beginnings
often create confusion.
Lord, you said that anyone who loses his life for you,
will find it again.
So, as I contemplate marriage,
help me to lose my self-centredness,
and find a deeper more God-like love within.
Give me eyes to see my partner in truth and love
and give me a life that will overflow
into new life for others.

LOVE AND COMMITMENT ARE NO MORE DIFFERENT
FROM EACH OTHER THAN FLAME IS DIFFERENT
FROM FIRE.

St Francis de Sales

Getting The Sack

I just sat there. It was only my second time in that office. The first time it was exciting and a new start. Today I was speechless, stunned,

I'm afraid we will have to let you go.

In one sentence my world had changed totally. They were letting me go. I hadn't finished my basic training. I had hoped to move up through the firm and make up for a below-par exam performance at the end of school. Now I was confused and lost. They had chosen me. They had not chosen any of the other three who started with me.

Everyone was very nice, but behind the glance of pity or the reassuring hug, what were they really thinking? I found it hard over the next month to get any energy to look for something else. All I had energy for was anger and I turned it on anyone who got in my way. I turned it in on myself too and began to feel I was a total failure. I began to drink too much and I went to bed to hide rather than rest. It took a month to realise that it wasn't only the firm that was letting me go, I was letting myself go as well.

LORD,
it's hard to cope with setbacks.
I know the logic of the business world, people cost money,
it's not personal.
So why do I feel so let down by this job loss?
I realise how much I relied on it only after I had lost it.
It gave me an answer to the questions at dances -
What do you do? What are your plans for the future?
Now I just have to shrug and say, I don't know.
I must look like one of life's losers to them.
And yet, perhaps I am a little wiser and freer.
There are opportunities to be explored,
and more to life than work.
Lord, I was beginning to let myself go,
when your hope slipped back in.
Thanks, Lord, for never letting me go,
when things change.

IT IS THROUGH WHAT HAPPENS TO US THAT GOD'S
WILL IS ALMOST ALWAYS RECOGNISED.

St Francis de Sales

A Bank Statement

This list of figures turns into a detailed map of my life. It tells me what time I took cash from the machine, where I was, and how much I took. It tells me what I earn, how I spend my money. That minus figure at the bottom of the column tells me I should be worried, I am living beyond my means.

A wise person once said, "Don't tell me what's most important in your life, show me your bank statement and that will show me your priorities." I wonder what my own bank statement shows? It shows I like to eat out a lot, and that I spend too much time on the telephone. I'm not saving, I'm just getting by on what I earn. I need to cut back on holidays if I want a new computer. Looking at my bank statement clips the wings of my dreams back to reality. It may not be the most popular monthly message I receive, but it tells me a lot about who I am and how I am living. I should sit and think about it more often.

LORD,
I can see the pattern now.
I can visualise the scene in the cafe each Friday night.
It's usually me who produces the plastic card,
and pays for the group.

Why do I do that?
Why do I feel the need to pay when I can't afford it?
Then, down the list, there's the payments on the new car,
bought three years ago.
Most of my friends bought second-hand;
not me, I'm still paying.
What am I doing Lord? Showing off? Buying friends?
I don't know.
All the shops I use are listed there too,
the same weekend pattern of trailing round clothes shops
searching for the right look.
Is that the way I really want to spend my weekend?
It looks a bit sad as I see each weekend fit the same
pattern.
Lord, perhaps if I spent my time differently,
I might spend money differently too.
If I got into sport, or got out-of-town at the weekend,
did a job or two for others,
then maybe I would be building up what you called
the treasure in heaven,
rather than being sucked into this spending madness we
call living.

USELESS WORRY CAN CREATE A DEADENING
OF YOUR INNER SELF.

St Francis de Sales

Working for Peace

I heard an amazing statistic today and I find it hard to believe. During the 20th century there was an average of over 40 wars going on at any one time! That makes it one of the most violent and destructive centuries in human history. I know that century is behind us now, that we can make a new start. But it's not that easy. The people from that century, still alive today, are affected by those wars. Their parents may have been involved, or scared, or guilty about what was going on. Palestinian children are still growing up not trusting Jews. People in Northern Ireland are still struggling with grief, Iraqis and Kurds will find it hard to live on the same street.

But what's all that to me? I'm just one person in the human race, what can I do? The answer has to be that I can only do a bit, but it's my chance to influence things for the better. I could join an organisation, I could contribute to fund raising for refugees. More personally I could stand up for justice where I am, defending the dignity of people. I could also check my own feelings too because I find it easy to blame whole groups of people for what is going wrong. Those children in the town centre, those greedy businessmen in our cities, double-talking politicians, they can all become excuses for me not doing anything. All that it needs for evil to grow is for good people to do nothing.

LORD

help me do what I can, with compassion and honesty, in dealing with my brothers and sisters at home and across the world.

MAKE YOUR CONVERSATION HONEST, GENTLE, AND SPONTANEOUS. WATCH OUT FOR THE EFFECTS OF MANIPULATION, PRETENCE AND HYPOCRISY IN YOUR OWN CONVERSATION AS WELL AS IN THE CONVERSATIONS OF OTHERS.

St Francis de Sales

My Gran

She's always there and she's got time for me. I'm glad we didn't move away when that new job came up for Mum. I even like the smell of her house, her photographs all around the shelves. It's like a family museum and she's the curator. She's saved my life a few times when I'd given up on Mum and Dad. I've nearly fallen off her big overstuffed sofa a few times, with things she's told me about Mum and Dad.

I never knew that Mum shaved her head when she was seventeen just to annoy my Gran, and as for coming in before 11 pm, they both had the same excuses as I give them today. Listening to Gran somehow calms me down. She puts things into perspective. She spins my story into the bigger family picture. She makes me feel I belong even when I'm not getting on with Dad and Mum.

It's not easy sometimes to admit that I am like Mum and Dad in my ways. I hate it when I do the kind of things they used to do when they were kids. But it's comforting too because they're alright really, if they'd only give me a little space to find myself. Gran keeps reminding me not to be too hard on them. She realises that if I am hard on them, I will be too hard on myself. I can't be totally different from them can I? Gran keeps telling me I have Dad's eyes and I have to learn to like that. Little does she know

I'm going to have my head shaved this weekend, then I'll have my Mother's haircut when she was seventeen. That'll give Gran a great laugh.

LORD,
thank you for Grandparents! For their wisdom and balance and for just being there.

LIVE GENEROUSLY AND WITH
A REASONABLE HEART.

St Francis de Sales

Long-Term Sickness

Most people get glandular fever and are better in a few weeks. I've been stuck in bed, on and off, for months now. I went to the post-box last week, two hundred yards away. Now I'm back in bed, exhausted. Just when you feel you're getting better this illness comes up and whacks you from behind.

At the start of the illness my friends were round every day. Then, as weeks went by, the visits became less and less. Now I get a couple of visits a week from just two friends. It's interesting how your friends change according to your needs. Some just don't know how to cope and others are just naturals. Most of the time I've been lonely, aching and tired, but I couldn't cope with visitors for long anyway. I can't read because my eyes are sore, and this fever seems to stop me thinking. I'm struck by how helpless we really are, and how dependent we can easily become. I was the tough independent type until I woke up one morning almost paralysed. Now I'm like a baby again and for Mum it was easy to slip back into caring for me as she used to. For me it was one hell of an adjustment!

I know I gave her a hard time but eventually I had to give in and I think I appreciate her more now.

Dad pops in occasionally for a longer chat but he's able to pick up the signs when I get tired of talking and listening.

LORD,
illness is a great teacher. I hope I can learn from it and not grumble about it. Stay with me through my weakness and frustration and help me to accept the frailty and the wisdom it can bring.

ACCEPT NOT JUST BEING ILL
BUT ALSO THE PLACE IN
WHICH YOU ARE ILL,
AND THE PEOPLE THAT ARE WITH
YOU WHEN YOU ARE ILL.

St Francis de Sales

A Better World

Global warming, air pollution, GM food! They're turning the world into a big chemical works to feed Industry. That's the way it seems. There's a poster in my room showing an old Indian Chief, reminding us how sorry we will all be when the last tree is cut down and our world becomes a desert. It digs into my mind each time I see it because his eyes seem to follow me around the room and asking when I'm going to do something about it. I do what I can. I recycle paper and glass. I keep up with the news on safer foods and Eco-friendly Products.

I remember a sermon where the priest said that in this world everything is part of everything else. I got quite thoughtful about that because it is so mysterious and at the same time its solid reality, my flesh and blood is part of everything and somehow I meet God through all that exists.

My friends looked at me as if I was totally mad when I told them about it. But they should wake up a bit. Two of them have got asthma because of what are called environmental factors which means chemicals in the air. We're all more likely to get skin cancer than our parents and who knows what stress will do to us over the years ahead. I do think it's worth struggling to keep life as natural and as simple as we can. But I also want to feed hungry people and develop new medicines. The need to make a better world is really important to me and I don't want to mess it up for anyone else.

GOD OF CREATION
help me to see you in the world. Help me preserve its goodness and beauty and explore the mystery of your presence within it.

GIVE AWAY SOME OF YOUR WEALTH
BY SHARING IT WITH THE POOR
BUT DO IT WITH A GENEROUS HEART.

Francis de Sales

Who wants to be a millionaire?

"I do!" most people will say, thinking that money will solve their problems. But recent research has proved that winners are no happier after winning a fortune than they were before. There's an old song our grandparents sang, "Who wants to be a millionaire? I don't, because all I want is you."

That song tells a different story, reminding us of the Beatles song, "Money can't buy me love." In the end it is love that we are made for, and love takes us deeper than happiness. Happiness depends on what happens, it makes us dependent on what goes on around us. Love helps us face deeper relationships, it helps us penetrate mystery and cope with joy and suffering. Who wants to be loved? Everyone! Anyone who is loved is already a millionaire, because they have touched that eternal quality that gives meaning to all of life. They have found a treasure within that no rust can destroy. They have caught heaven by the hem and touched the face of God.

LORD
help me not to be caught in the net of money, spending and saving it above all else. Help me to use money and not be used by it. Show me that people come first. Show

me that slowly building a world of love leads to a
richness that no bank account can contain.

NOTHING DONE IN A HUGE RUSH OR IMPULSIVELY
IS EVER REALLY WELL DONE.

St Francis de Sales

Bunjee Jump

I can't believe it! Yesterday I did a bunjee jump! Yes!
Me! Me, the scared pale-faced wimp who takes a first
aid kit to cross the road and an extra fleece if I go
over the third floor at work. It was amazing, I amazed
myself. I was so calm and just said "Yes", and just
trusted the man who was strapping me into the
harness. My brother waited down at the bottom with
a camera as the cage was hoisted high over the river.
I'd stood and watched for half an hour so I knew
what happened. They talk to you all the time as you
go up and as the cage stops and is tied off they do
one last check, open the cage door and you're on the
edge. The last thing you hear as you fall out is the
man shouting, "Enjoy it!" And I did! Just flying
through the air and feeling free. It was all so quick.
Hanging there I could see my brother clicking away
as I was lowered back to the mat. He was so proud
of me. I was proud of me too!

I wish Jo could have been there to see me fly!
Without that friendship I would not have had the
courage to go for new things. Jo has helped me fly in
ways more important than a bunjee jump. Her help
has been there when I signed on for that college
course and got through the interview. It was Jo who
kept me going when my relationship broke up and
kept me hoping for new friendships. I know that

since her car accident she can't get out of the house and I can't easily get to see her. I must let her know that her belief in me has given me wings and even from her wheelchair she continues to make a huge difference to my life. I will call to see her at the end of term, when I get home.

LORD,
thank you for the strength that comes through encouragement and the confidence that blossoms through believing in the inner resources within us all.

DON'T WISH TO BE SOMEONE ELSE,
JUST KEEP TRYING TO BE YOURSELF

St Francis de Sales

Gap Year?

I wanted to email Phil before I go off on summer work to give him time to think about taking a year off with me next year. I know it's a bit sudden but it struck me, listening to the guys here at college how easy it is to just slip into the pattern of work. Concerned only with bills and home, without having any adventure in life. This might be my last chance to do something different. I can almost hear Phil laughing. What will he think? It would be good to get away, out of the country and see how far our money will take us, and what work we can get. I'm getting worn out listening to my parents asking me about what jobs I'm applying for, what's my career path? They want safety, I want adventure.

We could pool our money, do up the car and just head off. He speaks a bit of French and my grandparents are Spanish. We could head out there first and see how we get on. I think I could earn a bit during my last year at college and extend my overdraft and build up a lump sum. I need to do this. I want to get out of the rut and live a little dangerously. I don't want to be safe or settle down, I want to be free and see what life has to offer before I settle somewhere. There's so much to see, different cultures, food, languages to experience. I feel this is almost like a vocation. I've got to do it, I'd hate myself if I didn't. I am sure there is something almost spiritual pulling me out into the poorer parts of the world.

LORD,
help me to resist dropping into a pattern that anaesthetises my spirit and always opting for safety. Give me the courage to find and trust my road and stay with me on the adventure of new experiences.

GOD OFTEN FIRES US UP WITH AMBITIONS
WHICH MAY NOT HAPPEN SO THAT WE CAN
EXPLORE THE POSSIBILITY
AND GROW IN SENSITIVITY TO GOD'S WILL.

St Francis de Sales

A Letter from Prison

Dear Alec,

I never thought you'd get a letter from me with a prison number at the top, I should have told you but I was sure I'd get away with community service but they have suddenly got very hard on dangerous driving. It's over six months since the accident and the guy I hit is already walking without crutches. They say he will always be in pain and he looked awful in court. I was really genuinely sorry for driving like a lunatic that day. In court I was dressed in my best suit, the one I wore at Liz's wedding. I was so sure it would be community service Alec. I nearly fainted when the judge said one year in prison and I don't mind admitting I cried. My job is finished, my family are ashamed, and I am a criminal. It couldn't be much worse.

As I left court, I was amazed to see a look of real concern on the face of the guy I ran over. It shocked me to the core. How could he care for me who had put him on crutches and into pain and finished his football career in one lunatic moment? That's why I'm writing Alec. Can you do me a favour, go and see him and take him a present, a book token or something from me. Tell him how sorry I am too and I will go myself when I get out. This is really important Alec, don't put it off for too long.

I never want to come back here again Alec. It's not just the smell of cabbage and urine, it's the hopeless sadness, the waste of life that kills your spirits. I nearly ended one man's life six months ago and I will pay the price. I value life and freedom more than ever before. Don't ever land yourself in prison Alec, and make that visit for me, please.

LORD,
help me accept responsibility and pay the price for the mistakes I have made. Help me to learn from mistakes and not repeat them.

As soon as anger against another person catches you out, balance it out with an equal act of kindness because fresh hurts are easier to heal.

St Francis de Sales

College at last!

I'm settled into the halls of residence and the course
has started. The theory is good and I recognise a lot
of the stuff even though the books are different. The
practical and professional placements are more
challenging, but I hate wearing a suit when I am
only nineteen – I feel a fool.

Here in the halls of residence the doors on the
corridor are left open and people are playing their
own brand of music into the corridor, desperately
hoping someone will go in and talk about music or
videos or anything. It's weird and lonely right now.
I've joined the climbing club and the French Society
just to meet people but the French Society never
materialised and the climbing club hasn't met yet.

In the evening the corridor slips into a desperate
attempt at party time. Everyone has a bit of money
and room-parties are happening all the time as
people try to get to know each other. I just lie here
missing my friends and comparing people on the
corridor and in lectures to my real friends back
home. People like Stef. I know in a few weeks some
friends will begin to emerge from this new situation,
people I can laugh with and be honest or stupid
with. But I will feel I am almost betraying my friends
back home when that happens. I feel more nostalgic
than adventurous right now as regards friends. I am

in a kind of limbo between two different patterns of friendship. I've taken to saying a prayer at night, I light a candle in my room as I study, to remind me of friends and God in my life.

LORD

keep close as my friendships change. Give me wisdom to make good choices and the patience to build relationships slowly. Be a friend to me in lonely times and help me to recognise the mysterious tug of genuine friendship when it comes along.

IN QUIET PRAYER, TALK TO GOD IF YOU CAN.
IF YOU CAN'T, JUST STAY THERE,
LET GOD LOOK AT YOU,
AND DON'T WORRY ABOUT ANYTHING.

St Francis de Sales

Out on the Hills

I went walking with some of the lads from down the pub. I came back aching. My knees won't go upstairs this morning! My Dad just laughed and told me to take a good soak in the bath. Which I did.

It wasn't the most adventurous of walks but it was enough for me. We did what Andrea called The Horseshoe. It was boggy at the start but we got into a good rhythm and I got chatting with Pete. You know him, he helps behind the bar sometimes. In the great outdoors he came across as more confident and outgoing – definitely more talkative than he is in the pub.

Anyway, Andrea noticed we were struggling a bit and slowed down. We discussed doing a shorter route but Alan was determined to do 'The Full Monty', as he kept saying. Actually he was well out of condition and his beer belly was a bit of a sight in his T-shirt. We argued a bit but Alan won the day – as he always does in the pub, and we did 'The Full Monty'.

But it cost me a lot and Andrea and Pete more or less took over the leadership. Alan and his friends bellyached a lot whereas Andrea and Pete were both really encouraging and decisive. At one point cloud covered us completely and we panicked. Andrea and Pete didn't turn a hair. They just pulled us together

and took a compass-bearing and carried on. I'd
always seen Andrea and Pete as a couple of
wallflowers. It just shows you how wrong you can
be I'm going to talk to Andrea and Pete a lot more!

LORD,
*help me not to judge people too quickly. Help me to see
deeper than the surface to the richness at the heart of
other people. Help me recognise and encourage the gifts
you have given to other people and recognise your
goodness in everyone.*

FOCUS YOUR SPIRIT WITHIN YOUR HEART EVERY
NOW AND THEN. THERE, IN THAT QUIET PLACE,
YOU CAN SPEAK TO GOD ABOUT YOURSELF.

St Francis de Sales

Discovering friends

I've been up all night talking with John. He told me last night that he was gay and it was really difficult for him to say it. I was the first one he had told and it was just like a dam bursting. He was so relieved to tell someone who didn't laugh or run away. I felt really privileged that he trusted me. I never realised how fragile and alone John had been feeling. I never guessed he'd been asking me out last year because he wanted to run away from being gay. We sat drinking coffee and realised he'd been in my bedroom until three in the morning and we laughed at what people might think and how wrong they would be. He cried and then he got angry in a confused way. While I tried to understand him, I felt out of my depth too.

He wanted me to tell Mike, and would like to talk to both of us at the weekend. He says he's always respected us, and our relationship. He said that he felt really safe with us when we were together. Our love could help him through. He really needs us and I'm glad my relationship with Mike might be a kind of harbour for him over the months ahead. Oh, I also ought to ask his forgiveness for spending the night with another man – but I'm sure he'll be glad I did.

LORD,
help me to have a listening heart and form relationships
that are open and supportive of others. Let the space
between me and my friends become a place where others
can feel safe. Be in that space to help and to heal hurts
where our experience and wisdom fall short.

GOD'S LOVE IS VERY HAPPY THAT WE SHOULD
HAVE OTHER LOVES.

St Francis de Sales

Rock Concert

I went down the arena with my older brother yesterday. There was a huge line-up of bands playing for six hours. It cost too much but it was absolutely brilliant! There was a group of ten guys who went with us on the train and we were buzzing before we even got there. Phil was doing cartwheels down the platform until the ticket collector shouted at him! We just laughed and pushed on through the barrier. Outside the station you could spot others on the way to the gig, and we laughed and joked with a few groups.

We met this bunch of guys from up north. They were absolutely amazing. They knew loads of lyrics to songs we knew. They had harmony lines and raps too that were better than we've heard anywhere. Turns out they play as a group just for fun, for themselves. It was great to meet them and they liked us.

But the crowd was all like that, really up for it, glad to be there. The noise was awesome; my bones were vibrating to the music. The whole crowd of heads in front of me rippled with the music. It was amazing to be part of it. I felt so close to everyone there. It was kind of spiritual, you know, not churchy, just beyond words.

LORD,

you said that you wanted us to have life and live it to the full. I hope that includes things like these rock concerts. I felt so alive and together with so many other people. It was as if we had all touched a source of energy that connected us deep down. If your kingdom is anything like that Lord, just bring it on!

HANG ON EVERY DAY TO THE HAND OF YOUR FATHER IN HEAVEN AND KEEP CHECKING TO SEE IF WHAT YOU ARE DOING PLEASES YOUR FATHER IN HEAVEN

St Francis de Sales

PRAYERS FOR THE ROAD

Our Father for the Road

OUR FATHER
Who walks with the millions of hungry people
of the world.
Who is in the lives of all who seek justice
because they love others.
Who is recognised in the faces of family and friends,
on life's journey.
Who is seen in the natural goodness and generosity
of ordinary people.

HALLOWED BE YOUR NAME
In all those who defend life and freedom,
to travel one's own path.
In the poor and humble,
who still have faith and hope in you.
In the ordinary moments of ordinary days,
made holy by your presence.

YOUR KINGDOM COME
Your Kingdom of freedom and love,
of fraternity and justice.

Your kingdom of rights and responsibilities,
of truth without deceit.
Your kingdom of joy and celebration
of the seasons of our lives.
Your kingdom in the network
of relationships that make up our communities.

YOUR WILL BE DONE

Your will that breaks down every burden
that oppresses humanity.
Your will that is to proclaim the good news to the poor.
Your will that brings comfort to the afflicted,
freedom to the imprisoned.
Your will that strengthens those
who have given up on the journey.

GIVE US THIS DAY OUR DAILY BREAD

The bread of a true freedom for all to be themselves.
The freedom to be in the house
or on the street without fear of violence.
The bread of equality, the bread of joyfulness,
the bread of your presence.

FORGIVE US OUR TRESPASSES

For not knowing how to share the bread,
that you have given us.
As we forgive those who have snatched from us
what is really ours.
Forgive us for separating ourselves from those in need.
Forgive us, Lord, for the lack of courage
to be living bread for others.

AND LEAD US NOT INTO THE TEMPTATION

To resign ourselves to compromises on the road.
To lose the clear vision that you want us to have.
To believe that nothing can be done.
To forget those we walk with on our journey.

BUT DELIVER US FROM EVIL

Of deceiving ourselves.
Of not recognising that we really are called,
to be our brother's keepers.
Of apathy of inaction.
Of not believing that our efforts can make a difference.

BECAUSE YOURS IS THE KINGDOM

Yours is the power,
and not any other person or organisation.
Yours is the wisdom and the glory
at the end of all journeys.
Because you are the only God, now and forever.
Amen.

When I'm lost on the Road

My Lord God
I have no idea where I am going.
I do not see the road ahead of me.
I cannot know for certain where it will end.
Nor do I really know myself,
and the fact that I think that I am following your will
does not mean that I am actually doing so.

But I believe that the desire to please you
does in fact please you.
And I hope that desire is in all that I am doing.
I hope that I will never do anything apart from that
desire.
And I know that if I do this
you will lead me on the right road,
though I may know nothing about it.

Therefore, I will trust you always
though I may seem to be lost
and in the shadow of death.
I will not fear, for you are ever with me,
and you will never leave me to face my peril alone.

Waiting on the Road

Waiting ....
Waiting for the kettle to boil.
Waiting for the phone to ring,
the end of the day,
the mark for the essay,
the next bus,
the pay cheque.

We wait for letters,
for holidays,
for signs of friendship,
for promotion,
for the end of term,
for forgiveness.

We wait for everything that is really worth having.
We wait to be born,
for love to touch us,
for life to grow,
for healing of hurts,
for a turning point on the road.

Lord teach us to wait,
on your wisdom, on your timing,
and on your methods.

Help us to surrender our self-importance
to the freedom of trusting in you.
Amen.

A Sporting Prayer

Lord, help me to be sporting.
In the game of life help me to give my best,
and tackle others well and safely.
Teach me not to over-react when I am challenged.
Keep me cool and focussed on the game.
When the opposition seems tough,
help me work harder with my team.
Keep me aware of their struggles and not just my own.
Make me always ready to encourage,
to forgive and start again.
Teach me to celebrate success when the goal is scored,
and help me recognise that we did it together.
When the time comes to be substituted,
or to change position,
help me do so with good grace,
recognising that others need the chance to play the game.
Whatever others do, help me to play by the book.
When decisions are unfair and referees unrepentant,
help me to avoid anger and red cards.
At times I know I will get hurt in the game,
help me be realistic about my injuries;
neither getting back too soon,
or sitting fearfully on the bench too long.
When the time comes for me to hang up my boots,
and stand on the touch-line,

help me to accept that watching,
supporting, and advising is part of the game too.
When the final whistle blows,
may I end the game knowing that I have played well,
played fair and joined a team that will last forever.

When I can't get to Church

(This meditation follows the pattern of the Eucharist. You might want to try lighting a candle and playing some appropriate music.)

Gathering
Lord, I want to gather in my mind all those who have touched my life for better or worse during the last week. I can imagine their faces, their words and the events we have shared and I realise you have been present through it all. (Pause)

Forgiveness
I recognise that the last week has not been perfect and I need to accept some responsibility where I have made mistakes in what I've done and not done. (Pause)

Counting Blessings
God's mysterious presence has been hidden in the events of my life and I want to recognise that and count the blessings of the last week. (Pause)

Prayer

Lord, you have promised to be with me always. Thanks for staying with me last week, in all that has happened. Help me keep looking for you in the people and events of next week, so I can find your wisdom and mystery deep in the life of everyone I meet, and in me! Amen.

Listening to the Word

Think of your favourite story from the Gospel. Put yourself into the story and talk to God about its message for you for the week ahead. (Pause)

Intercessions

Think of those who are in need. Let your prayer reach around the world. Pray for the planet, for its people and for those who suffer. (Pause)

Offering Prayer

Lord, I give you my life, my worries, my dreams for next week. I put my plans and my difficulties, my family and my relationships into your hands. I trust you to make sense of what will happen to me in the week ahead.

An Act of Self Consecration

Lord, join my life to your life. Help me see that every week brings its own fragments of death and resurrection. Help me to see that pattern of dying and rising working in me. Join my life to your life pattern so that I can let go of whatever traps me and be open to new life, new people and new ideas. Then I will live through you, with you, and in deeper unity with all those around me.

Silent Communion

Be still and aware that God is in you, with you, knowing you as you are. Like two people who know each other well, just sit with God who knew you before you were even born. In your mind just sit looking at God looking at you. (Pause)

Final Prayer

Lord, prepare me to meet this week in your presence. Help me to do good wherever I can and leave the world a better place. Help me remember to talk to you each night and until we meet again next Sunday.
Amen.

Being a Friend on the Road

Maintaining good relationships
◆ Let people know you care about them.
◆ Make the first move in opening conversation.
◆ Look for the mystery of God's presence in all people.
◆ Be optimistic about people's goodness.
◆ Praise and encourage often.
◆ Try to put yourself into the other person's world and understand their situation.
◆ Have a personal word with people regularly.
◆ Be ready to laugh at yourself.

When things go wrong

- Calm down and don't panic.
- Listen carefully and look the other person in the face.
- Try to sort out what's gone wrong by good questions.
- Never criticise someone in public or in front of friends.
- Never isolate or ignore someone for long periods.
- Don't ever use sarcasm.
- Leave the person aware that you are open to continued friendship.
- As far as possible, forget the problem and return to a friendly approach.

Based on the Advice of Saint John Bosco

What I Believe

I believe that I have a purpose.
I believe that I have a dignity simply because I am here.
I believe that I can make a difference to the world around me,
and leave the world a better place.

I believe in a presence that is mystery, that is God.
I believe in a presence that moves in my own heart.
I believe that in friendship, in forgiveness and in love,
I am touching that mystery in other people.

I believe I am called into action by God.
I believe in a gospel that challenges me to grow.
I believe that the process of dying and rising
is being worked out in the daily pattern of my own life.

I believe that this mystery is eternal.
I believe my life is safe within this mystery of love.
I believe that I will live forever in that love,
as it was lived out in the life of Jesus Christ.

The Lord is my Friend on the Road

The Lord is my greatest friend,
I shall try not to be afraid.
God leads me towards safety and goodness,
and through struggles to a deeper inner peace.
Near relaxing and refreshing streams,
God consoles my anxious spirit.
He surrounds me with goodness,
all the way into eternal life.
In the sight of people who have written me off,
He is preparing a celebration that will last forever!
In His home I will be alive
with the amazing life of God.
Goodness will surround me all the way into eternal life.
God has marked me out as a friend,
and my life already overflows with that relationship.
If I should slip into deep anxiety or pain
God is with me.
His goodness surrounds me all the way into eternal life.
If I become depressed or frightened,
I will trust God even more.
As a guide through death and into life,
God is keeping me safe in an eternal friendship,
that will pull me through all difficulties on my road,
and into eternal life.

Based on Psalm 23

A meditation when Worried

Don't get worked up about future disasters that may never occur anyway. When and if they do occur, God will give you the strength to bear them. Jesus asked Peter to walk on water, but Peter became afraid and almost drowned. If God asks you to walk on turbulent water tomorrow, do not doubt, do not fear, because God is with you. Forge straight ahead, treading the path that is nearest in order to live the day well, without worrying about the final one.

Too often we spend our efforts trying to be perfect angels instead of good women and men. Our failings will accompany us to the grave. We cannot walk without touching the ground; and if it is true that we must not give in or lie down and do nothing, it is also true that we must not try to fly without wings. We are not meant to be angels. So live each day humbly, gently and lovingly in partnership with your God. Do not be worried, put behind you the memory of small failings by admitting them honestly. Try not to be upset about the difficulties of the day, but bring your mind back to the presence of God and have confidence in the compassion you find there. Stay close to God and he will lead you by the right hand on the road.

Based on St Francis de Sales

Mantras for the Road of Life

Most spiritual traditions use repeated phrases called mantras to help connect with a deeper spirituality in the busyness of life. You can make your own up and repeat them quietly in your mind on and off during the day. They can be simple ways of maintaining a relationship with the mystery of God at the heart of everything.

Here are some mantras based on the words of Jesus in the Gospel:

- Do not be afraid,
- I am with you always.
- Do not worry about tomorrow.
- Peace I leave with you
- I am your loved son/daughter with whom you are well pleased.
- Lord, make me gentle and humble of heart.
- The kingdom of God is among us.
- Your will be done.
- Jesus I trust you.
- I bless you Father
- Lord, help my unbelief
- Lord that I may see
- Lord have mercy on me
- Jesus I need you

Common Gospel Prayers

OUR FATHER, WHO ART IN HEAVEN,
hallowed be thy name.
Your kingdom come, your will be done on earth,
as it is in heaven.
Give us this day our daily bread.
Forgive us our trespasses,
as we forgive those who trespass against us.
And lead us not into temptation,
but deliver us from evil.
For yours is the kingdom,
the power and the glory for ever and ever.
Amen.

HAIL MARY FULL OF GRACE THE
LORD IS WITH YOU.
Blessed are you among women,
And blessed is the fruit of your womb, Jesus.
Holy Mary, Mother of God, pray for us sinners now,
and at the hour of our death.
Amen.

LORD I AM SORRY,
FOR ALL MY FAILINGS,
and the faults that break the trust
between me and others.
Forgive me Lord,
for the way I have ignored your friendship.
Help me to put right what has gone wrong,
and live closer to you in the days ahead.
Amen.